Rani of Jhansi

Sayanti Mukherji

Rani of Jhansi

First Edition: August 2009
64 Pages
Printed in India.

ISBN 978-81-8493-233-1
Pro-ya-en-53

Prodigy Books
177/103, First Floor,
Ambal's Building, Lloyds Road,
Royapettah, Chennai 600 014.
Ph: +91-44-4200-9603

Email : support@nhm.in
Website : www.nhm.in

Prodigy Books is an imprint of New Horizon Media Private Limited

Contents

The Saga of Bravery

'We record our homage and deep admiration for the Womanhood of India, who in the hour of peril for the motherland forsook the shelter of their homes and with unfailing courage and endurance stood shoulder to shoulder with their men folk, in the frontline of India's national army, to share with them the sacrifices and triumphs of the struggle.'

This quote about the Indian women taken from one of the resolution's passed on January 26, 1931, showcases the reality behind the Indian freedom struggle. Acknowledging the priceless contributions and sacrifices made by the women of India, many prominent leaders remarked that 'when India's fight for Independence is written, then the sacrifice made by the women of India will undoubtedly occupy the foremost place.'

Glancing back in to those days of freedom struggle only reiterates the active participation and selfless sacrifice of numerous great women of our country. There was a particular period when the British imprisoned almost all the prominent male leaders of India to curb the freedom struggle. Out of the helplessness of seeing their leaders behind bars rose a huge wave of protest.

A protest, that was just not ordinary but the most remarkable happening that had re-written the saga of Indian Independence struggle. The wives, mothers and daughters, who till then silently bore the burden of reality came forward and took charge of the struggle, revealing the real power of the normally subdued, shy Indian women.

This sudden turn of events took not only the British, but also our own leaders by surprise. It was then, the whole world knew that freedom struggle was just not a man's movement but belonged equally to our tenacious women too.

Women's participation in the freedom struggle, began in 1817, when the brave Bhima Bai Holkar fought and recorded a historic win against the huge army lead by the British Colonel Malcolm. Following her foot steps, came another brave lady, Rani Channamma of Kittur who faced the mighty army of East India Company in 1824.

As the list just goes endless, the first name that comes to mind when one thinks of Indian freedom struggle is none other than that of Rani Lakshmi Bai, the queen of Jhansi. Considered as an epitome of bravery, integrity and leadership, Rani Lakshmi Bai set an unprecedented example for all the future women freedom fighters of India.

Who was this firebrand leader? Would she have become as famous as she has if it weren't for the circumstances she lived under?

In all probability, if the annals of time hadn't opened the way it did, Rani Lakshmi Bai would have continued life as an aristocratic widow and queen of 19th century India, till such time her adopted son came off age to inherit the throne. But destiny forced her to take a different road all together, in the form of annexation of her State Jhansi.

Forced to turn in to a rebel, Rani Lakshmi Bai fought till her last breath to save her annexed state of Jhansi from the ruthless rule of the British. Dressed as a man, whenever she entered the battlefield, holding the reins of her horse in her mouth and handling her sword with both her hands, she gave a tough time and sleepless nights to her enemies during the battle.

With a resolve to fight back as long as she could, she lead her troops with undaunted courage to give a befitting reply to all those who caused agony to the people of Jhansi.Although beaten, she refused to surrender to the British and fought valiantly till she dropped dead.

Not only the Indians but also the British acknowledged her as 'the best and the bravest rebellion' in the history of Indian freedom struggle, who died a hero's death in the battlefield, fighting the enemy till her last drop of blood. Fondly remembering her sparkling bravery and sacrifice for saving her state and the country, every Indian proudly says,

'Khoob ladi mardaani vah to jhansi vaali raani thi'

- She fought like a man; she was the queen of Jhansi

Early Days

Born in 1828, in Varanasi, to Moropant Tambe a Maharastrian, Kharade Brahmin and his wife, Bhagirathi, Lakshmi Bai was originally named Manikarnika, also known as Manu to her family and friends.

Her father, Moropant Tambe was an advisor to Chimnaji Appa, brother of the last Maratha Peshwa, Baji Rao II. Her mother, Bhagirathi was a woman of great learning and wisdom. Unfortunately, when Manu was four years old, she was permanently bereaved from the love of her mother due to Bhagirathis sudden and unexpected death. Loss of his wife left Moropant with the responsibility of bringing up the motherless child alone.

The absence of a son and being the only child, a motherless one too, reflected greatly on the manner in which Manu was brought up. She was brought up in manners customarily associated with boys and became a tom-boy, bold and fearless, leaving behind all the traces of conservative upbringing.

Her fathers position ensured that Manu spent her childhood in the court of the Peshwa where she learnt to read and write including Persian. She also learned elephant and horse riding, as well as sword-play, target shooting and handling other kinds of weapons.

At the age of seven, Manu was promised in marriage to Gangadhar Rao Newalkar the widowed Maharaja of Jhansi. In 1842, her father traveled to the court of Jhansi to get her married to the Maharaja. Their marriage was celebrated pompously amidst great fire works and canon salutes. Known for her bold nature and witty character, she is said to have instructed the priest who presided over the marriage to tie the knot tightly. It was after her marriage, at the time of pronouncing her as the queen of Jhansi; she was given the name Lakshmi Bai.

Her husband, Maharaja Gangadhara Rao had little interest in state affairs as he was more inclined to theatre and the patronage of music. One year after his wedding, he allowed Lakshmi Bai to govern the affairs of the state. In 1851, though a son was born to them, the child unfortunately died when he was just four months old.

Gangadhara Rao, who was childless by his first wife, could not recover from the loss of the only son born to his second wife. The fact that he had no heir became a constant cause of worry to him due to which he soon fell very ill. As his condition deteriorated, Lakshmi Bai suggested adopting a child of distant relatives. Though Gangadhara Rao refused initially due to his failing health, he agreed to adopt Ananda Rao, a four year old child, who was later renamed as Damodar Rao. Soon after the adoption, Damodar Rao was declared as his successor and the heir of Jhansi.

To ensure that the British would not be able to contest the adoption, the Rani had the ceremony witnessed by the local British representatives, the Political Agent, Major Ellis, and Captain Martin. At the same time, a will was prepared requesting the British to treat Damodar as the true son of Gangadhar Rao and stating that Lakshmi Bai would be regent till Damodar Rao came off age to inherit the throne. The will was read to Major Ellis, and repeated in a letter to the Political Agent for Gwalior and Bundelkhand, Major Malcolm.

On 21st November 1853 Gangadhar Rao died making Lakshmi Bai the ruler of Jhansi.

Rani Lakshmi Bai

The queen of Jhansi

Rani Lakshmi Bai was aged twenty six when she was widowed and became the ruler of Jhansi. Within no time, she proved that she was not just another queen but an astonishing woman and ruler born before her time. As soon as she took the throne, she cast aside many conventions to unite people of all castes and religion, she cut across the social norms of her time, and refused to accept her fate as a woman.

Personally too, as a widow, she didn't cut her hair but wore it knotted at the back; and she dressed and rode like a man. She put aside the purdah system and encouraged other women to do the same. She added a women's wing to the army of Jhansi. Usually the zenana (women's quarters) were guarded by armed women, who occasionally took part in battles; but it was unusual for the Rani to be in charge of their training. She won the affection of the people of Jhansi, her subjects and soldiers who called her 'Bai' lovingly.

Though she dressed like a man with a turban, which she thought was more appropriate for a warrior queen, behind the façade of a man; she was a woman who adored jewellery. She wore diamond bangles and a large diamond ring on her little finger. She also carried a short jewelled sword and two silver pistols which were always stuck in her cummerbund.

Born as a Brahmin woman and brought up almost like a man, she balanced her acts accordingly as and when the situation demanded. As a devout, Hindu, Brahmin lady she performed daily puja and adhered to all the rituals that had to be followed by a lady of her position. At the same time, as a warrior queen, she did not hesitate to touch her soldiers, as a sign of comfort if the situation demanded.

Those were the days when a woman, that too a widow would have her chastity questioned if she dared to look at another man even if it was a wounded soldier. But Rani's lifestyle was so impeccable that no one had the courage to slander her name. Much respected and loved by her people and her soldiers, she cared for them equally and consulted with them on all crucial matters and carried them with her. To her contemporaries and even to her enemies she had magnetic charm and appeal. She was a leader who led from the front.

Though she had a larger than life personality her humility knew no bounds. A learned Jhansi Brahmin who escaped the massacre of the city after its fall related that few days later as he was wandering across Central India trying to hide from the chasing soldiers, he found himself beside a well where he decided to rest a while. Soon he noticed a group of riders with the Rani amongst them galloping towards him. When the group dismounted, the tired, dusty and dishevelled Rani asked for some water. Though the Brahmin rushed to serve her, recognising him, she stopped him saying that a man of his learning shouldn't be serving her, and instead helped her self.

So large hearted she was, that even while dying her thoughts were for her subjects. After she was fatally wounded and removed to a mango grove, she distributed her priceless jewellery amongst her attendees who were with her before dying. This final act of the Rani proves that she had a rare personality that was a combination of undeterred courage and true magnanimity.

The Doctrine of Lapse

Lakshmi Bai was confronted with British hostilities very soon after inheriting the throne. The then Governor General of India, Lord James Dalhousie took a decision to ruthlessly implement the Doctrine of Lapse to annexe princely states under the banner of the East India Company. Just like pawns in the game of chess, the princely states of India, fell defence less to the Governor General's shrewdness and British imperialism one after the other.

The princely state of Satara was the first to be annexed in 1848, followed by Jaitpur, Sambalpur and Nagpur in 1849; and finally in 1854, the British turned towards the State of Jhansi to annex it too.

It was through the Doctrine of Lapse that the British were able to capture almost the whole of Northern India. If one has to know what exactly the Doctrine of Lapse and its working was and why it had caused much resentment amongst so many Indian rulers, forcing them to rebel, one has to go back to the times when the British entered India as mere traders.

On a cold Dec 31 evening in 1600, a Charter was passed by Queen Elizabeth I confirming the formation of The East India Company. Eighty British traders wished to trade, through that company, with India and Far-East Countries. In 1608, following the charter, a delegation of British merchants arrived in Surat, Gujarat. India extended a warm welcome because the British were not the first traders to the subcontinent. Much prior to them, the Arabs started their trade relations with India as early as the 7A.D and continued to trade for generations since then. As the time passed by, the Arabs settled down in India and considered it their home.

But unlike the Arabs, the intentions of the British were purely to trade with India and they were prepared to employ any means fair or foul to achieve this end. India was never a home for them. The Doctrine of Lapse was one such tool of expansion and acquisition.

Being the 14th Governor General of India, Lord Dalhousie was appointed to administer and govern the Company's three provinces of Calcutta, Bombay and Madras. Known as the "builder of the British Empire" Lord Dalhousie was associated with The **Doctrine of Lapse,** an annexation policy that was so vexing and controversial that it has been accused of being the primary cause of the mutiny of 1857.

Though Lord Wellesley, in the 18th century brought several Indian states under British dependency through his Subsidiary Alliance, Lord Dalhousie only took it a step further, and insisted that by the Doctrine of Lapse, territories under dependency of the Subsidiary Alliance, would automatically be annexed if the ruler was either "manifestly incompetent or died without a direct heir".

19th century India was the perfect canvas for exercising such a land-grabbing ploy, with more than 650 immensely wealthy princely states or kingdoms. Under an ancient Hindu custom, to avoid dispute at the time of succession, a ruler with no born heir could adopt a male of any age from another branch of the ruling family and appoint him as his successor.

Lord Dalhousie, who found it opportune to expand the British Empire, had neither the sympathy nor the will to understand and respect the Indian traditions. Using the Doctrine of Lapse as a weapon against all such princely states that had no direct heir, Lord Dalhousie vetoed the succession of an adopted heir and annexed the princely states, one after the other.

However, the adopted successor and heirs were allowed to keep their titles and an annual maintenance allowance was allocated to them. Thus, advocating the Doctrine of Lapse, Lord Dalhousie annexed many states and successfully added approximately four million pounds sterling to the Company's annual revenue.

In Jhansi's case, money and land grabbing wasn't the motivation. Jhansi was only about 2600 sq miles with negligible taxes but its location was unique. Situated in the midst of several other districts of Bundelkand, which were already in British possession, the annexation of Jhansi would only regularize the administration of these states. In spite of several justifications by the British, the annexation of Jhansi was perhaps most unfair because Jhansi had been pro-British since 1817, when Ramchand Rao the grandfather of Gangadhar Rao signed a treaty with the British.

Rani's Statesmanship

Though Damodar Rao, who was then, a mere boy of 5 to 6 years was the legally adopted son of the late Maharaja and Rani Lakshmi Bai; the British rejected the claim that he was the heir to the throne. Instead, Lord James Dalhousie claimed that as the Raja had died without a male heir, the kingdom of Jhansi could not continue as an independent sovereign and ordered to annexe it in February 1854.

Nullifying her son's adoption and annexation of Jhansi came as a double blow to the Rani. Lord

Dalhousie not only took over Jhansi politically; but by not accepting the adoption of Damodar Rao, he also inflicted a personal insult to the soul of the Raja. According to Hindu law, the heir is responsible for performing the 'after death rites' to ensure that man's soul reaches salvation. It was as if the Raja died heirless with no one to perform his death rites, thus depriving him of eternal salvation.

It was then, that Lakshmi Bai put her political skills to test. She did the most unexpected and unprecedented thing by choosing to appeal. She represented her case through several letters to Lord Dalhousie against the annexation. Her letters are highly noted for their sound and rational arguments.

On Dec 3rd 1853 through the local Political Agent Major Robert Ellis, she wrote her first letter, referring to the adoption. She emphasised that it could not be questioned as it was performed as per the rules and also reminded Lord Dalhousie that British officials had been present to witness the ceremony. But to her surprise, the Rani had not received any reply even after a wait of two months.

Not leaving the matter there, Lakshmi Bai appealed again through another letter and forwarded the same on February 16th 1854. In it she mentioned the history of Jhansi, its close ties with the British and also referred to the Treaty of 17th Nov 1817 according to which the British Government had to not only recognize the natural offspring of Raja Ram Chand Rao, the ruler then, but also his 'successors' as 'the hereditary ruler'. She also wrote that the lapse represented a "gross violation and negation" of this treaty.

Her 3rd appeal was drafted upon the advice of British counsel, John Lang, who was in India at that time and had had some success against the Company in the courts of London. There followed an appeal, at considerable cost, first to the Court in Calcutta and then to the Directors of the Company in London. Although these petitions were well-argued, they were ultimately rejected. Dalhousie brushed away all her arguments and pleadings, totally unaware of the power of a scorned woman and the grave consequences that were to follow.

Lord Dalhousie was considerably irritated by her persistence, more so because he could not deny her logic. Out of spite, after the second letter, he decided to settle the Raja's personal property in favour of the son, rather than his widow. Interestingly, his action only proved that Lord Dalhousie considered Damodar Rao, the legitimate heir for the Raja's personal property, but not for the throne. Undeterred, the Rani continued to write to Lord Dalhousie till 1856.

In spite of her relentless efforts, five months after the death of Gangadhar Rao, in May 1854, Jhansi lapsed to the Company. Lakshmi Bai, who was then aged 26 years, was pensioned off at an annual pension of Rupees 60,000 and was allowed to keep only her personal palace. The Raja's troops were disbanded and replaced by soldiers of the East India Company. The Rani was left with no choice but to abdicate the throne.

Anyone else less determined would have admitted defeat but Lakshmi Bai continued her fight with any tool at her disposal. She refused to take the pension, on the ground that it would amount to accepting the annexation of the state. However, she was persuaded to change her mind by Mr. Lang, her lawyer, who was deeply sympathetic to her predicament. Once she agreed, she was informed that the British expected her to repay her husband's debts to them, out of her pension. Perhaps this was the punishment for her audacity to appeal to the courts of London. The British confiscated the state jewels and deducted her husband's debts of Rupees 36,000 from the pension.

Not only that, Lakshmi Bai was forced to leave Jhansi fort for the Rani Mahal in the town. But Rani Lakshmi Bai was as stern as she could be and publicly expressed that she was not ready to give up her claim to Jhansi. She proclaimed her decision with words that have now become immortal and had been etched in the Indian history forever;

'Mi mahji Jhansi nahi dehnar'

—I will not give up my Jhansi.

The Revolt of 1857

By the time the revolt of 1857 broke out most leaders of North and Central India were vexed with the high-handedness of the East India Company, the root cause being the Doctrine of Lapse. The common people too, had their share of grievances as a few economic and social changes the British tried to impose on the Indians were not welcomed by them. However, the immediate cause of the revolt was quite dramatic, which is referred to as the "greased cartridge incident".

British soldiers looting a city in 1858

It so happened that the British Government decided to replace the old heavy Brown Bess smooth-bore musket with new Lee-Enfield rifle in India. Loading the new rifle required extracting from a pouch, a cartridge with a greased patch at the top, which had to be torn off with the teeth and then rammed down the barrel.

The sepoys believed that the grease used for the purpose was made from the fat of cows and pigs. This was sacrilege to both Hindus and Muslims. The news spread amongst the sepoys of various regiments causing unrest and anger, as a result of which, the Indian regiments refused to accept the greased cartridges. Starting first at Dum Dum ammunition factory in Calcutta, the unrest spread to other factories and infantries, too which stood firm on their word, refusing to use the greased cartridges.

In March 1857, a young officer named Mangal Pandey revolted when he was forced by the British to use the cartridge against his will. Out of rage, he fired at his British Adjutant and Sergeant-Major, also calling upon his fellow sepoys to join him. After wounding both the officers, Mangal Pandey was caught and hanged immediately, which resulted in more unrest. Soon, the revolt had spread all over like a wild fire.

The real trouble started in Meerut on the evening of 9 May, 1857. On that evening, when 86 sepoys refused to use the greased cartridges; they were dismissed and sentenced to 10 yrs of hard labour. As a result of the harsh action against the sepoys, on 10 May 1857, three regiments broke into open mutiny; broke open the prison door, released their compatriots and began to march towards Delhi. On their way, they were also joined by the common folk. Soon, from Meerut the rebels moved to Delhi, marking the beginning of the revolt of 1857.

In Delhi, the civil population led by Bakht Khan, joined the sepoys. They captured Delhi within two days and re-installed Bahadur Shah Jafar, the last Mughal ruler as the symbolic head of the uprising. The siege of Delhi lasted from July 1 to September 21. The Company soldiers made a base on the ridge located in the north of the city and laid seige to the city. For much of the siege, the Company forces were outnumbered and it seemed that it was the Company forces and not Delhi that was under siege. On August 14th the Punjab Regiment under Sir John Nicholson arrived as reinforcement.

From September 7, the siege guns battered breaches in the walls and silenced the rebels' artillery. On Sept 14 the Company forces stormed the city through the Kashmiri Gate. They suffered heavy casualties, including Sir John Nicholson who succumbed to his wounds. After a week of street fighting, the British reached the Red Fort. The British had retaken Delhi and proceeded to loot the city. Bahadur Shah Jafar was found hiding in the Humayun's tomb and was taken into custody. His sons were shot, while he and his wife were exiled to Rangoon where he died in prison 1862.

Since the recapture of Delhi, Lucknow, the ancient capital of Oudh, became a centre of resistance for the mutineers. Led by Begum Hazrat Mahal and joined by the Hindu and Muslim Talukdars, the common people rose in revolt. In

May 1857, they captured the Residency, where the English along with Sir Henry Lawrence and General Neill had taken refuge and within 90 days of the siege, the rebel army was successful in reducing the number of men in the Company forces from 1700 to 1200.

In September, though a relief column under the command of Sir Henry Havelock and Sir James Outram fought its way from Cawnpore (present day Kanpur) to Lucknow, it was unable to break the siege. Instead they were forced to join the garrison within the Residency. Then, a larger, army under Commander-in-Chief, Sir Colin Campbell, came for rescue and relieved the English officers from the siege. Later, in 1858, Sir Campbell once again advanced on Lucknow; and drove away the large but disorganised rebel army from the city with few casualties to his own troops.

When rebellion broke out on June 5, 1857, the besieged European entrenchment including women and children who were unprepared for an extended siege, surrendered to the rebel leader Nana Saheb in return for a safe passage to Allahabad. However, during the evacuation things went out of control and most of the men were killed. The women and children were captured and later executed, in what came to be popularly known as the Bibighar Massacre.

Soon, the Company forces reached Cawnpore under Brigadier General Neill and captured the city. On July 19, General Havelock occupied Nana Saheb's palace without resistance. After a struggle of four months, in November 1857, Nana Saheb with the help of his ablest general, Tantia Tope, recaptured Cawnpore. However the rebels were defeated by the Company forces under Sir Colin Campbell in the Second Battle of Cawnpore, marking the end of the rebellion in that area. Tantia Tope then, joined Rani Lakshmi Bai, after the sudden disappearance of Nana Saheb, who was believed to have fled to Nepal.

It is believed that in Gwalior and Jhansi, Rani Lakshmi Bai led the revolutionaries. Though the sepoys of the Company rebelled at the fort in Jhansi immediately following the Meerut revolt, Rani Lakshmi Bai was still apprehensive about joining the rebel forces. But due to the sudden, violent changes in the situation, she was coerced to transform in to a rebellion, in order to protect her State. It wouldn't be an exaggeration to say that the role of a rebel leader was thrust upon her.

The Rani, a reluctant rebel

Soon, the Great Indian Mutiny gathered momentum and raged on endlessly. In June, 1857, the sepoys of the East India Company rebelled against their British officers in Jhansi for the first time. Later, things followed in such way that Rani Lakshmi Bai was drawn into the rebel camp much against her will. When the sepoys first revolted, Lakshmi Bai still remained faithful to Jhansi's treaties with the British, by which they had appointed her as their agent after the annexation. She fulfilled this obligation in spite of her personal bitterness towards the British for disinheriting her son.

She aided the rebels only at the point of their guns, and immediately informed the British so that they were aware that she was being forced to aid them. When the rebels forcefully extorted money from her, she told the British "*What can I do? The sepoys have surrounded me....to save myself I have sent them guns and my followers*".

Apart from the reason she made evident to the British, there was another reason why she supported the mutineers, against her will. The reason being, the mutineers threatened to reinstate Sadesho Rao Narain, a distant relative to the throne if she didn't support them. Fearing that she would loose the little hold she still had over the administration of Jhansi, she rendered her support reluctantly.

The mutineers were boisterous and uncouth; many of them were nothing more than dacoits and convicts released from prison. A point came when the threat to her life was so imminent that with British's permission she appointed, for her personal protection 150 guards. In spite of her helpless situation, she invited the British soldiers and their families to come and stay in the palace when she knew that their barrack at Star Fort outside the city limit was in danger of attack. When they refused to do so, as an alternate measure, she sent her attorney and 40 men from her personal guard to protect them.

On June 8th nearly a hundred European men, women, and children were treacherously massacred at Jokhan Bagh by the rebels who had allured them from Star Fort with the promise of safe passage out of Jhansi. On one hand, it is strongly believed that Lakshmi Bai cooperated with the officers and offered shelter to them in her palace, although in the end she couldn't protect them from the ultimate massacre and on the other hand, there is also a rumour that, motivated by revenge she invited the families to her palace so that they would be ambushed and killed en-route.

Though she was initially defended by the British as a 'ruler caught in an unenviable situation' who had been forced to aid the rebel, later the British accused her of instigating the mutiny. Despite sufficient evidence that the mutineers had forced her to assist them, the British officials in Calcutta chose not to believe her from then onward.

Shortly after the mutineers left for Delhi, Lakshmi Bai shouldered the responsibility of restoring law and order in the state. She again wrote to the British expressing her loyalty to them and asked them for their aid to Jhansi. But the British, who were by then totally convinced of her involvement in the massacre of Jokhan Bagh, did not respond to her letter.

As she was about to establish a peaceful reign in Jhansi, adding to her already existing troubles, Sadasheo Rao Narain, the usurper to the throne attempted a coup, that came as an unexpected blow to the Rani. But finally the coup was easily foiled and he was taken prisoner. Alas! Little did she know then that more trouble was in store for her from her aggressive neighbours, Datia and Orchha?

In September and October of 1857, Jhansi faced invasive attacks from her neighbouring states of Datia and Orchha. The forces of Orchha laid siege to Jhansi between the 3rd and 22nd of October whilst claiming to be acting for the British. Under the able leadership of Lakshmi Bai, the army of Jhansi was able to defend their state from the threat of invasion.

From the tough experiences she faced one after the other, from unexpected quarters; Lakshmi Bai gradually learnt the art of general-ship. She concentrated hard on improving the army and defences of Jhansi. For strengthening her forces, she was also obliged to seek help from the rebels, who were the only force that could provide her with the requisite military aid. Though reluctantly, turn of events and her destiny forced her to prepare for the final confrontation with the British.

The British ignored her pleas for help in defending Jhansi and in turn questioned her motive of enlisting fourteen thousand soldiers. They also accused that her real reason was aggression against them. It was soon made apparent that the British did not trust her anymore and planned to tackle her at the first opportunity.

Having lost their confidence and fearing that Jhansi was in grave danger, she finally decided in favour of revolt and prepared to confront the British. Only if they had believed her, Lakshmi Bai would not have joined the rebel forces and history would have been quite different.

Once she was committed to protect Jhansi from the Company forces, Lakshmi Bai immediately undertook the task of building the city's defence. She prepared for war by moving back into the fort of Jhansi.

The city walls were repaired and strengthened; new men were recruited and placed into position. Women were also given military training. The bastions and turrets were manned day and night; the big guns were readied for firing. Six new large guns were manufactured, apart from the old guns that were already available. About 200 maunds (7460 Kilograms) of salt-petre was purchased from the district of Gwalior and brought to the fort of Jhansi. Gunpowder was daily made within the fort. Eight gunners from the Moorar rebels were sent from Kalpi into the service of Jhansi. Lalu Bakshi, seasoned gunner and explosive expert, was entrusted with the manufacture of brass balls and other ammunitions on a war footing.

Hundreds of tons of rice, grain were roasted and stored for ready distribution during the expected siege. Flour, ghee, sugar and other eatables were stocked for the troops and citizens. Available silver was sent to the mint to be melted down and turned into currency. Messages were sent to Rao Saheb and Tantia Tope for help. In this way, the courageous woman, undaunted by the oncoming storm, stepped forward to fortify her beloved city of Jhansi.

The siege of Jhansi

It was in January 1858 that Sir Hugh Rose, with two brigades opened his Central Indian campaign from Bombay. He began his advance on Saugor in Central India, which was under rebel occupation for seven months; till it was relieved by Sir Hugh Rose on 3 February 1858. With Saugor under his belt Sir Hugh Rose turned his attention towards Madanpur and on 3 March, 1858 forced his way through this town inevitably clearing his path to Jhansi

Back in Jhansi, Lakshmi Bai waited for the British. Eleven thousand men formed the garrison and the

Rani was accompanied by her brave warriors; like Gulam Gaus Khan, Dost Khan, Khuda Baksh, Lala Bhau Bakshi, Moti Bai, Deewan Raghunath Singh, Deewan Jawahar Singh and childhood friends Sunder-Mandar and Kashi Bai. She also had the huge support of the local population, who stood by her side, irrespective of their religion and caste.

When the British first sighted Jhansi, they saw the fortress standing on a high rock, built of solid masonry, with guns peeping between the ramparts. The city spread for four and a half miles in circumference around the fort, and was surrounded by a massive, eight feet thick wall. To the east of the city were a picturesque lake and a palace of the Late Raja. On the south side were the ruined cantonments of the British troops.

Though she was given the opportunity to surrender Jhansi, Lakshmi Bai refused to do so, because she knew that most of the sepoys she had recruited were mutineers and would have been executed by the British, if they surrendered.

On March 22 1858, Sir Hugh Rose opened the siege of Jhansi fort with relentless cannon shelling, but the Rani's troop stood firm and undeterred. In the Jhansi army, women were given the duty of carrying ammunition, repairing the damaged walls and supplying food to the soldiers. Rani Lakshmi Bai personally inspected the defence of the city.

Finally on March 29, the forts guns were silenced and the next day a breach was created in the outer wall of the fort. Soon a party of Bombay engineers stormed the breach and after heavy losses, secured a position allowing reinforcements to pour in. The breach only signalled the end of its first phase, the battle was far from over.

When all seemed lost, the following day hope arrived in the form of Tantia Tope and a party of more than 20,000 rebel forces to the relief of Jhansi. The news was greeted with shouts of joy from the walls of the fort and bonfire was sighted burning fiercely late into the night. But unfortunately, the help came in a little too late.

With the arrival of Tantia Tope Sir Hugh Rose was forced to split his forces between his two foes. But as the rebels were unable to capitalize on this division of forces, on April 1 Tantia and his huge rebel army were defeated at River Betwa, a few miles east of Jhansi by mere 1500 men of the Company forces.

After defeating Tantia's relief troop Sir Hugh Rose turned his attention back to Jhansi and ordered the Company troops to storm in to the Jhansi fort on 3 April 1858. As the British army entered Jhansi city, Rani Lakshmi Bai, dressed as a man took up arms and defended every inch of the city in house-to-house fighting; but the Company forces continued to advance.

When the situation went out of control, on the same night Lakshmi Bai decided to leave Jhansi. Despite Sir Rose's best effort to foil her escape; prior to the dawn of 4 April, she slipped out through the Bhanderi Gates of the outer walls of Jhansi with a small party of men including her father. With little Damodar strapped to her back, she made her way to Banda or Bhander. Though the British forces chased her, the Rani and her followers gave a tough fight to the forces. In spite of the forces killing most of her men, the brave, determined woman escaped them and rode towards Kalpi, which was a hundred miles away from Bhander. So amazing was her speed, that the distance was said to have covered by her in just twenty four hours.

On April 6, 1858 Jhansi fell; Sir Hugh Rose entered the fort. More than two weeks of hard fighting finally won the fort for the British. The flag of The East India Company was unfurled above the fort ramparts for the first time.

Though the total casualties on both sides were estimated to be about five thousand, the victims of the terrible atrocities, the British forces unleashed after the surrender of the fort ran in to huge numbers. Jhansi citizens who perhaps took up arms to protect themselves from looting Company sepoys were not even spared. Gallows were constructed at every street corner and men were strung up while women and children were left hapless. Captured Sepoys were often blown up by cannons.

The Battle Continues

The battle moved a little away from Jhansi to Kunch. On 1 May 1858, rebel forces under Tantia Tope gathered at Kunch, where Sir Rose confronted them. By series of clever manoeuvres Sir Hugh Rose forced Tantia to withdraw without a fight, thus admitting defeat. Lakshmi Bai joined hands with Tantia Tope and they retreated to Kalpi, north-east of Jhansi, with Sir Rose in hot pursuit.

The Rani reached Kalpi, only to find the rebel's morals low after their defeat at Kunch. But soon they were heartened by the arrival of Lakshmi Bai,

Rao Sahib, nephew of Nana Saheb and the Nawab of Banda. She lifted the spirits of the rebels by promising to fight with them to the end. Determined to make a stand at Kalpi, Lakshmi Bai and the Nawab of Banda feverishly prepared for Sir Hugh. Finally on 22 May, the rebels attacked the British forces outside the fort of Kalpi.

At Kalpi a decisive battle was fought. Once again Sir Hugh Rose out-manoeuvred the rebel troops. In addition, superior handling of artillery and last minute change in tactics confused the rebels and ensured victory for the Company troop, with minimum casualties. When the defeated rebels abandoned Kalpi, Sir Hugh Rose occupied Kalpi without any opposition. The battle of Kalpi was really the beginning of the end; but though Sir Hugh Rose had the fort, he still did not have Lakshmi Bai.

The rebel troop retreated and regrouped 60 kilometres southwest of Gwalior at the town of Gopalpur also known as Godalpur. Having been repeatedly defeated, they had little left by way of men and equipment but still they took a dramatic decision, which could only have come from Lakshmi

Bai. They decided to attack Gwalior, solidly defended by the British vassal Maharaja Jayjirao Scindia.

On 30 May, a large contingent of rebels advanced on Gwalior. On June 1 they were met by Maharaja Jayajirao Scindia, at Morar, outside the Gwalior fort, ready to flee as his garrison refused to fight. Protected only by his bodyguards, Maharaja Scindia fled to Agra and the fort fell. The impossible had happened!

The rebels had succeeded in capturing Gwalior the strongest fortress of Central India. Its treasure and fighting men were now at their disposal. There was a great deal of celebration; the rebel leaders proclaimed Nana Saheb as Peshwa. Lakshmi Bai was given the famous and a priceless pearl necklace from the Gwalior Treasury. The British were stunned at the loss of this strategic fort, which stood in the way of the 3 British armies from linking up; the third advancing from Bengal.

Though the capture of the Gwalior fort was truly an amazing opportunity, the rebel leaders could not put their victory to use as they were busy in celebrating Nana Saheb's coronation as the Peshwa.

Lakshmi Bai fretted and fumed and also tried her best to divert their attention to the task in hand, but to no avail.

Mean while Sir Hugh relentlessly continued his advance towards Gwalior, in the scorching June heat of Central India. At Morar Cantonments outside Gwalior, the fiercest battle was fought between 11 and 18 June, 1858. Unable to stop Sir Hugh at Morar, the male rebel leaders appealed to Lakshmi Bai to save them. It was then, Lakshmi Bai was given the command of the eastern flank, the most difficult to defend. Without ado, she led the last remnants of her Jhansi troops and the Gwalior contingent, which had given her its unflinching loyalty, and met the British at Kotah-ki-Serai on 17 June, in an effort to defend the mountain pass to the fort and city.

The last Battle

By then, Lakshmi Bai had been battling the British for four months continuously. Little did she know on that fateful morning when she woke up, that it would be her last day on this earth? That she would never return to her beloved Jhansi and instead her end would come on the hard dusty ground outside the fort of Gwalior. Perhaps she did. Certainly, someone as intelligent as her knew the mutineers never had chance against the Company forces. She had never wanted to take on the Company forces in a battle. Since the battle with Orcha and Datia, she was aware of the limitation of her own soldiers and knew they lacked professionalism to match the British. The only thing going for them was courage, but she was also well aware that courage alone doesn't win a war.

'Dressed as man', she rode out to battle with undeterred courage and valour. She wore the red uniform of a cavalry officer with a white turban and her hair tucked away. A Queen she was, she also wore her bangles, anklets and the regal pearl necklace gifted to her after the capture of Gwalior.

The Company troops attacked the pass, counting their advance in inches as the Rani refused to give way. Though the rebels were outstandingly brave and patriotic, their resources could not match that of the Company forces; and at last the 8th Hussar Regiment under Captain Heneage made a cavalry charge. The Rani met it unwaveringly, and in the subsequent encounter, was cut down, either by a cavalryman's sabre or by a bullet or both.

There are several accounts of her death, which hugely vary from one another. How she died, where, and when, is uncertain. While one version unfolds that she was killed on the parapets of Gwalior in a hail of gunfire at the beginning of the siege, others put forward that she died at Kotah-ki-Serai.

It is mostly said that she was knocked from her horse by a bayonet or sword and in retort shot at her attacker but missed. He, in turn, allegedly shot her, failing to realize who she was because she was dressed in men's clothing. This version is perhaps the most accurate, for Lord Canning too gave a similar account of her death in his report and is considered the most credible. There are also reports that say that she was not killed instantly, but was removed to a mango grove where she distributed her famous jewels to her subordinates.

In another version about her death, it is said that The Rani's original horse had been mortally wounded during the battle and had to be replaced by a less trained horse. During the battle, as she was trying to escape, two British officers followed her. The horse reached a cliff and being insufficiently trained, could not pass over it. Upon realizing that she was surrounded, she jumped off the cliff. A Brahmin found her at the bottom where she lay there unconscious for few moments and died uttering "Jai Hind!". Her servants cremated her body.

Her childhood friend, Sunder Mandar who stood by Bai through out her life, too died with her. The Rani's funeral was carried out very quickly since there was no guarantee that the body would be dealt with proper respect if the British found it.

Two days later, the rebels, demoralised by the death of Lakshmi Bai, left Gwalior making no attempt to hold onto what was virtually an impregnable position. The fort of Gwalior was retaken by the British. To all intent and purpose the rebellion was over.

Later, Sir Hugh Rose wrote about his foe; "The Ranee was remarkable for her bravery, cleverness and perseverance; her generosity to her subordinates was unbounded. These qualities, combined with her rank, rendered her the most dangerous of all the rebel leaders."

The Aftermath

Rani Lakshmi Bai's other maid of honour Kashi Kumbin, prepared the Rani's body for the funeral pyre. Kashi Kumbin along with another close attendant also looked after Damodar for two years after her death, before surrendering him to the British but only after a extracting a promise of safe custody for the child.

Damodar Rao was granted a pension by the British and lived a moderately peaceful life, though he never received his inheritance. Lakshmi Bai's father

Moropant Tambe was wounded while escaping Jhansi with her after the fall of the city, and managed to reach Datia where he was captured and handed over to the British. They hanged him with others at Jokhan Bagh as a revenge for killing the British officers and family at the very same spot when the revolt first started in Jhansi

The Revolt of 1857 ended the rule of the East India Company in India. The Government of India was taken over by the British Crown and Parliament. The India Council, under a Secretary of State and 15 members of the Cabinet were created to supervise the Indian administration. The Governor-General received the additional title of 'Viceroy'. Lord Canning became the first Viceroy of India.

Queen Victoria of Britain was declared the Empress of India. In 1858, the Queen issued a proclamation. "The Queens Proclamation" assured a change in British policy towards India. The British annexation policy was controlled and the Doctrine of Lapse was cancelled. Though the already annexed states were not restored, no new states were enfolded under the Union Jack.

There was also a change in the policy of the Government of India towards the Indian Princes. The loyalty of the Rajputs, the Marathas, the Sikhs and the Nizam had prevented the spread of the revolt. As a reward, their territories were guaranteed and some even received material recognition for special service. Perhaps the most significant change was psychological. Men like Lord Mayo and Lord Lytton now saw these princes as props of British imperialism in India. The people were assured of religious toleration and equality in matter of employment. A general amnesty was awarded to all rebels except those convicted of killing British officials.

In the army, the number of British soldiers was increased and all the important departments were placed under the British officers. Each department now consisted of sepoys belongings to different regions, religion, and caste, preventing them from forming a cohesive group within the army. In short, they began to follow a policy of 'division and counterpoise', or the policy of 'Divide and Rule' not only in the army but in all matters.

The legacy of the Rani

Rani Lakshmi Bai became an icon of India's independence movement against British imperialism in the 20th century; an emblem of India's freedom struggle. Her courage and bravery became so legendary that in 1943 Netaji Subhash Chandra Bose named the women wing of the Indian National Army after her, as the 'Rani of Jhansi Regiment'.

Statues of her are found all over India; the most famous being the bronze statues at Jhansi and Gwalior portraying her on a horse wielding a sword. Buildings, streets, housing colonies are named after her and school children are taught her story of courage, wisdom and selflessness. Even in 21st century India, her name springs to mind, every time one is confronted with a determined and brave woman who is referred to as "Rani of Jhansi"!

She was more than a martial leader. She was an astonishing woman born far ahead of her time; her progressive views on women's empowerment in 19th century India influenced many in the 20th century and still continue to do so.

And Jhansi, can she ever forget her? Lakshmi Bai's name has been intrinsically linked with Jhansi and had been etched in Indian history forever. As the Rani never abandoned her, neither can Jhansi ever abandon her most loyal daughter.

Prodigy books

Biographies

Abdul Kalam
Charles Darwin
Marie Curie
Visvesvaraya
Srinivasa Ramanujan
Newton
Einstein
James Watt
Jagdish Chandra Bose
Alexander Graham Bell
Gandhi
Jawaharlal Nehru
Mother Teresa
Ambedkar
Bhagat Sigh
Tipu Sultan
Rani of Jhansi
Akbar
Shivaji
Bharati
Martin Luther King
Alexander the Great
Napoleon
Adolf Hitler
Charlie Chaplin
Walt Disney
Bill Gates
Narayana Murthy

Classics Retold

Homer's Iliad
The Odyssey
The Tempest
Hamlet
The Merchant of Venice
Twelfth Night
Romeo and Juliet
Macbeth

Other Titles

The Universe
Hinduism
Global Warming
Abraham Lincoln
The New 7 wonders of the World
Life
Tsunami
Dinosaurs
Ganga
World War II
Madras - Chennai
Exam Tips
The Internet

www.ingramcontent.com/pod-product-compliance
Ingram Content Group UK Ltd.
Pitfield, Milton Keynes, MK11 3LW, UK
UKHW040003200726
13854UKWH00001B/18

9 788184 932331